May your candles burn bright

and your celebration be joyous.

May your table be filled with good food,

surrounded by family and friends.

Enjoy reading this true story of Hanukkah.

Experience a new family tradition

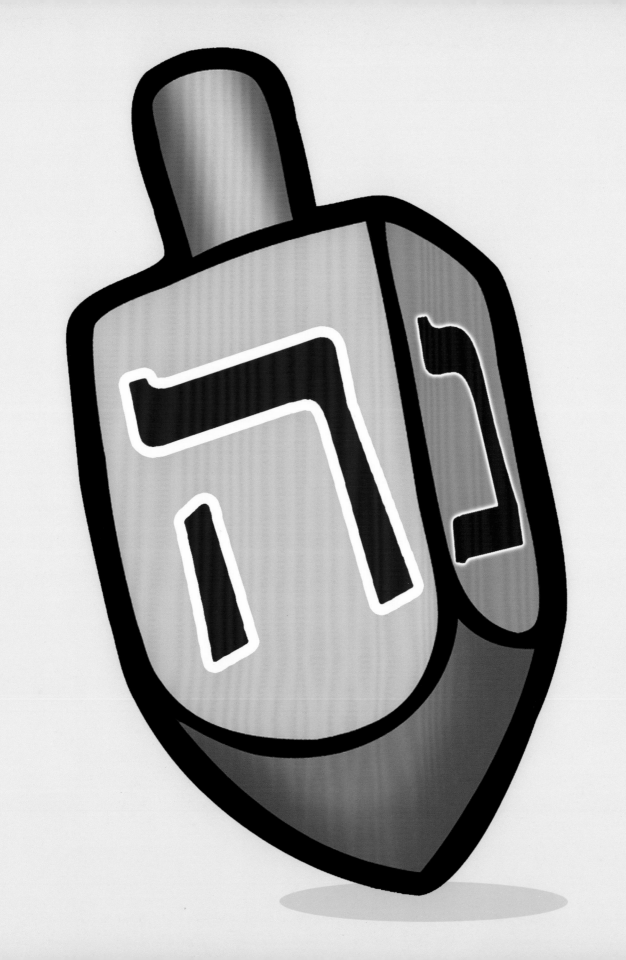

Gather around as this little Maccabee tells you the story of Hanukkah.

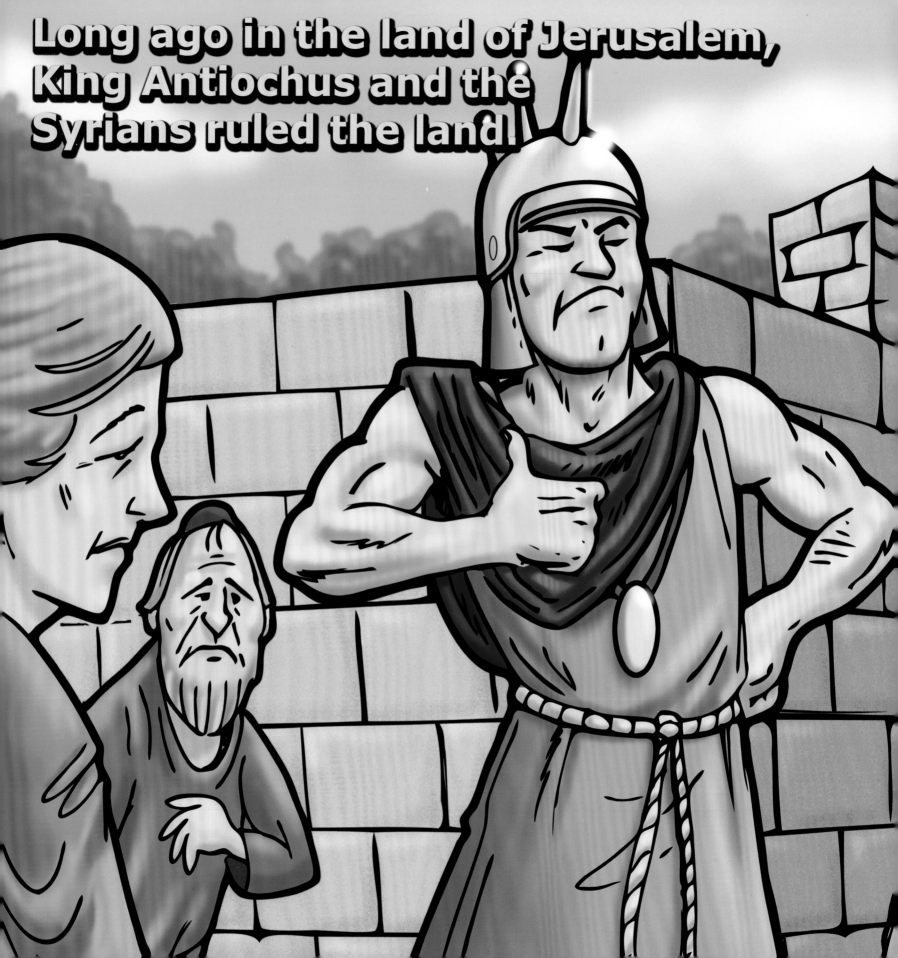

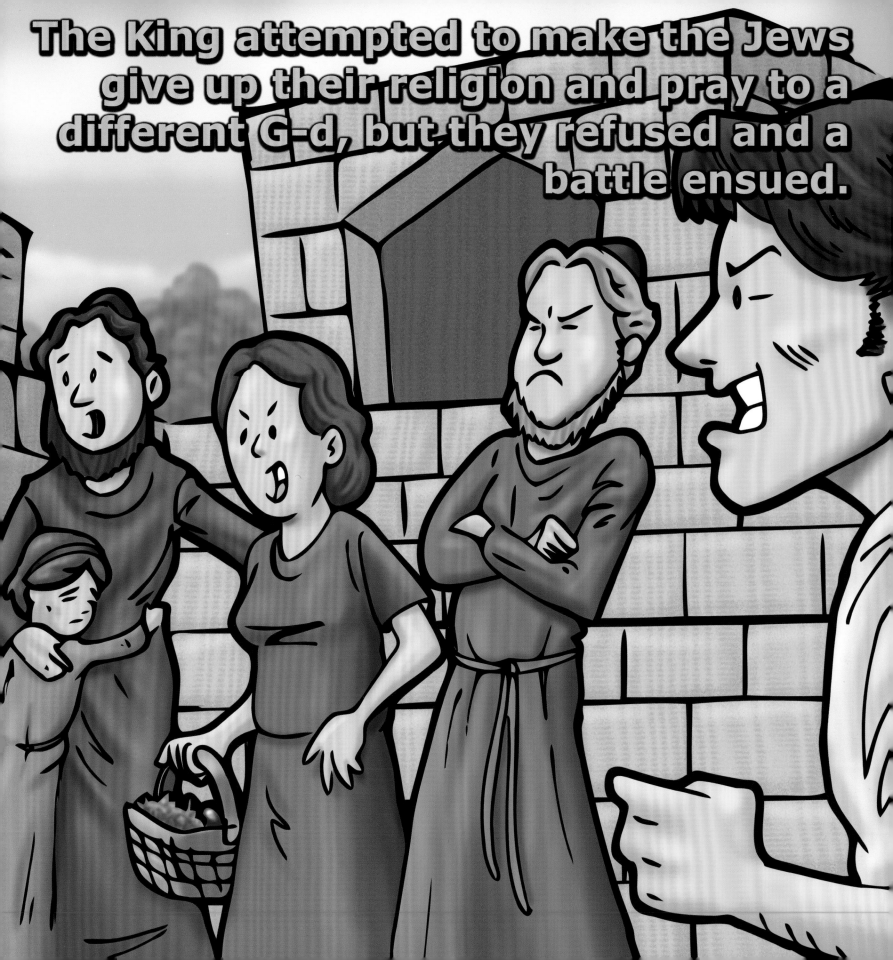

A young warrior named Judah Maccabee rallied his family and friends and miraculously defeated the much larger army of the Syrians.

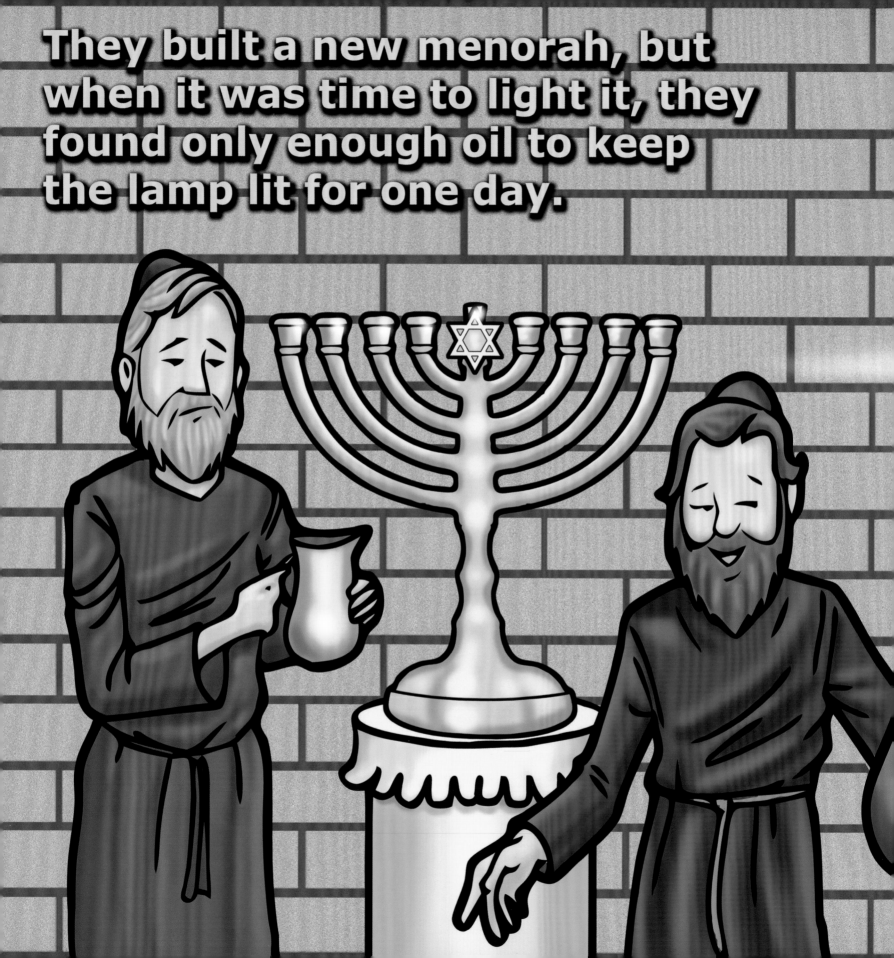

That is how Hanukkah became known as the Festival of Lights, because it celebrates the miracle that happened with the menorah.

Today we celebrate the Festival of Lights by enjoying potato latkes and jelly donuts during this eight day holiday.

We light the menorah in a special way.

On the first day of Hanukkah, three blessings are said with the lighting of the first candle. On each day after, only the following two blessings are repeated.

The first Hanukkah blessing is recited on all eight nights just before lighting the candles:

Baruch atah Adonai, Eloheinu melech ha-olam, asher kid'shanu b'mitzvotav v'tzivanu l'hadik ner shel Chanukah.

Blessed are You, Lord our G-d, King of the Universe, Who sanctified us with His commandments and commanded us to kindle the Hanukkah light.

The second Hanukkah blessing is recited on all eight nights just before lighting the candles:

Baruch atah Adonai, Eloheinu melech ha-olam,she-asah nisim la-avoteinu, bayamim haheim ba'zman hazeh.

Blessed are You. Lord our G-d, King of the universe, Who performed wondrous deeds for our ancestors, in those days, at this season.

The third Hanukkah blessing is recited only on the first night just before lightning the candles:

Baruch atah Adonai, Eloheinu melech ha-olam, shehecheyanu, v'kiyemanu, v'higi-onu laz'mman ha-ze.

Blessed are You, Lord our G-d. King of the universe, Who has kept us alive, sustained us, and brought us to this season.

On each night for eight nights, starting on the right side of the Menorah, we add one additional candle. However, we light the candles from the left to the right.

(Example: second night, two candles, light the second candle first.)

Let's count the candles, but don't count the *Shamash* candle.

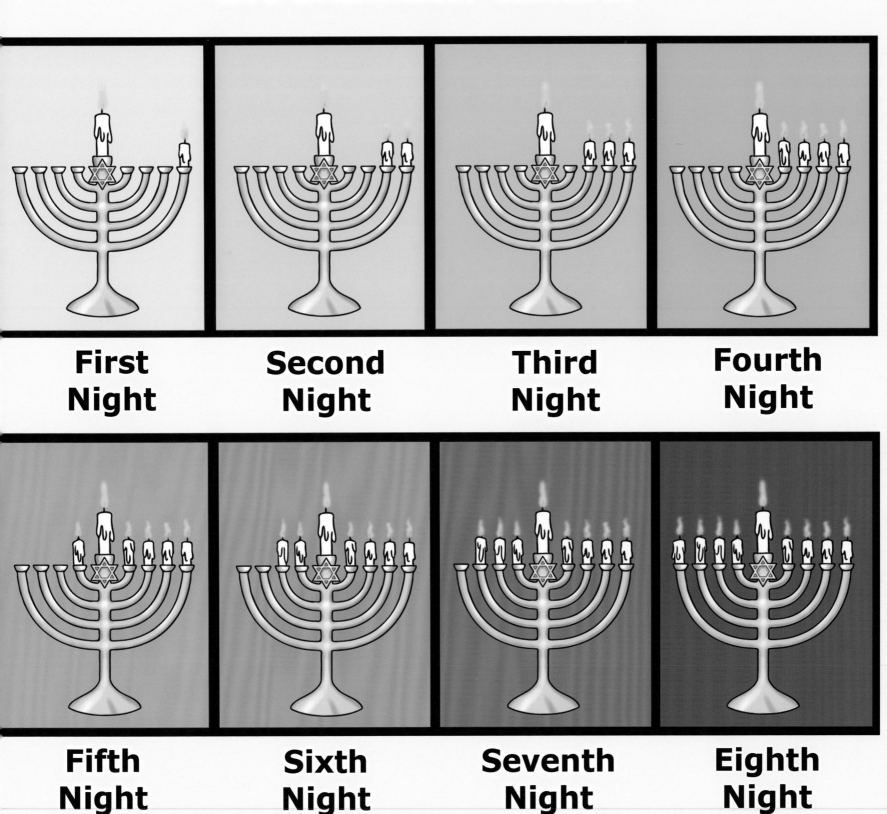

| First Night | Second Night | Third Night | Fourth Night |

| Fifth Night | Sixth Night | Seventh Night | Eighth Night |

When all the candles are lit it is customary to sing *Maoz Tzur.*

Ma-oz Tzur Y'shu-a-ti Le-cha Na-eh L'sha-bei-ach
Ti-kon Beit T'fi-la-ti V'sham To-da N'za-bei-ach
L'eit Ta-chin Mat-bei-ach Mi-tzar Ha-mi-na-bei-ach
Az Eg-mor B'shir Miz-mor Cha-nu-kat Ha-miz-bei-ach

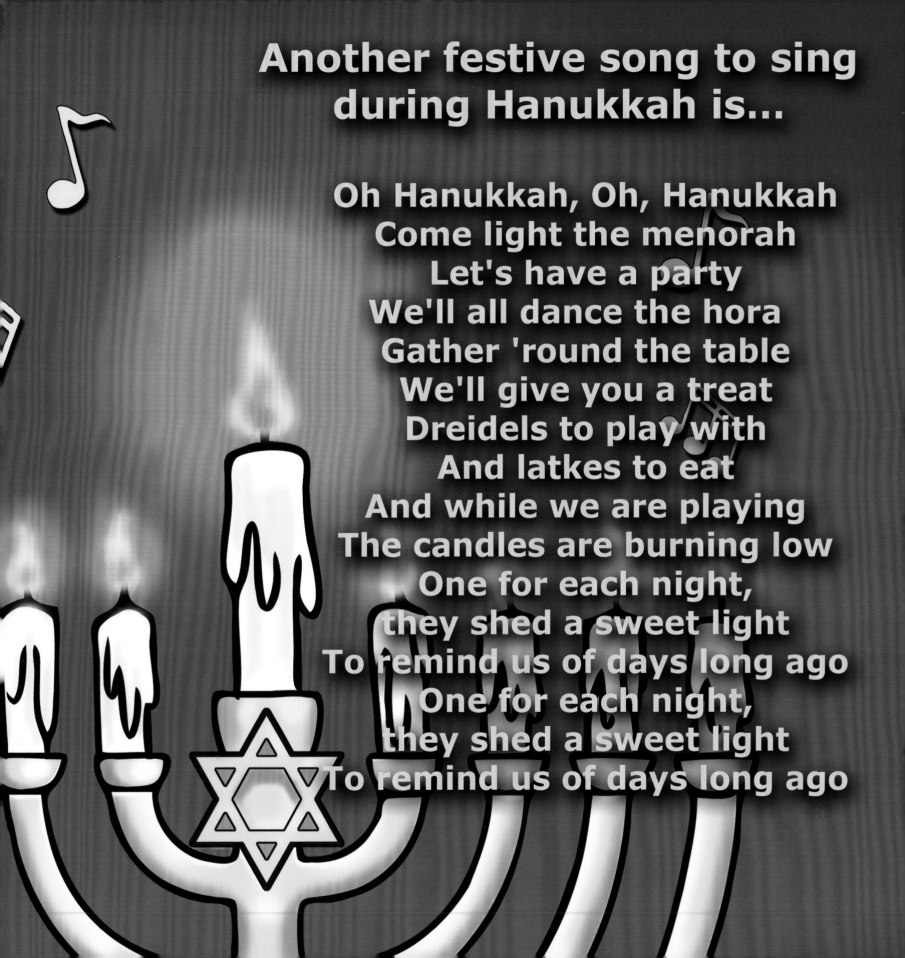

Another festive song to sing during Hanukkah is...

Oh Hanukkah, Oh, Hanukkah
Come light the menorah
Let's have a party
We'll all dance the hora
Gather 'round the table
We'll give you a treat
Dreidels to play with
And latkes to eat
And while we are playing
The candles are burning low
One for each night,
they shed a sweet light
To remind us of days long ago
One for each night,
they shed a sweet light
To remind us of days long ago

Children of all ages enjoy playing with the dreidel and singing this song...

I have a little dreidel. I made it out of clay.
And when it's dry and ready, Then dreidel I shall play!
Oh dreidel, dreidel, dreidel, I made it out of clay.
And when it's dry and ready, Then dreidel I shall play!

SHIN
The Player
Adds One Piece
in the Middle

HEH
The Player
Gets Half
from the
Middle

Each side of the dreidel has a Hebrew letter which tells you what to do when you play the game.

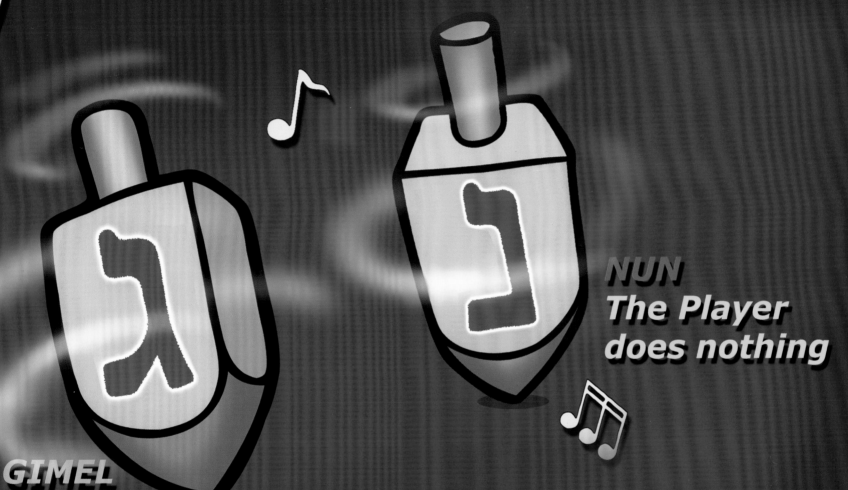

**NUN
The Player does nothing**

**GIMEL
The Player Gets Everything from the Middle**

These four Hebrew letters are the first letters of the Hebrew phrase "Nes gadol hayah sham" which means, "A great miracle happened here."

Hanukkah
Glossary of Words

Chag Sameach – Hebrew meaning Joyous Festival or Happy Holiday.

Dreidel - a small four-sided spinning top with a Hebrew letter on each side.

Jelly Donuts – a deep fried, jelly donut eaten during Hanukkah; or better known as a sufganiyot.

Judah Maccabee – a young warrior who rallied his family and friends and miraculously defeated the much larger Syrian army.

King Antiochus - the King of Syria, who reigned from 3538 to 3574 (222-186 B.C.E.)

Kislev - the ninth month on the Jewish calendar. Hanukkah begins on the 25th day of Kislev

Latkes – small potato pancakes which are shallow-fried pancakes of grated or ground potato, flour and egg.

Maoz Tzur – (Rock of Ages) a Jewish poem. It was written in Hebrew, and is sung on the holiday of Hanukkah, after lighting the festival lights.

Menorah – During Hanukkah, we use a Hanukkiyah, which is a nine-branched candelabra lit during the eight-day holiday.

Nes gadol haya sham – the four Hebrew letters on the dreidel spell out this phrase, which means "A great miracle happened there."

Shamash candle – sometimes called the "helper" candle that is used to light all the other candles and/or used as an extra light.